For Linda

Thank you for me & supporting me along the way! ♡

me drawing a picture of me[n]

July 2019

Rachelle Escamilla

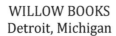

WILLOW BOOKS
Detroit, Michigan

me drawing a picture of me[n]

Editor: Randall Horton
Cover art: "Robert Burns Boyfriend Angle" by Naomi Edwards
Author photo: Lisa Robinson-Ward

ISBN 978-1-7322091-3-8
LCCN 2019937026

Willow Books, a Division of Aquarius Press
www.WillowLit.net

Printed in the United States of America

For Scott

...poor bitch, be wise.
—Robinson Jeffers

Contents

Summer

This is the time of day when men
thirty-three and thirty-two wear
slick business suits with horned lilac
blossoms in their pockets.

It's a sort of feeding frenzy
for walkers, wine drinkers. Fellows!
Let your hair grow long—no—
bald and vulgar.

Out of our sweet emails, you come.
Oh! Pittsburgh misses you today—
she told me. It was noon in front
of the red doors with black bolts -

the church on the edge of Ellsworth.
Not me. Pittsburgh misses you today.
She told me w her disembodied arms
and bobbling breasts. She whispers in
my ear as I cross the street at Ellsworth

and Clyde.

Dear Mister G,

This faulty form of communication is rendering my life—
finding you between the lines /
clicks of the mouse—

a muse is all I ask for.

Here I am searching this city for fundamentals but finding lost
words like:
        beauty, sublime, or *lascivious innuendo.*

By my memory, Mister, we grabbed each other under the neon
window:

brown legs   white calves   black hair

Today   three times I thought of your name.
It's circular topography.

You think of time and use logic.
I think of time and tell you

       Pittsburgh misses you

and you say

       I have so little time these days.

Where are we tonight?

Here in Pittsburgh, there are buses that run from downtown to
Oakland at all hours of the night.

     Tonight!

Where are we, tonight?   I find myself contemplating
                                                       cormorants.

From the sound of it, the Pacific is too far away tonight.

Here—

our fingers teeth together
like your zipper
and then not

Running in the park is the same w or w/out you.
I saw three different birds, *no*, they haven't flown south for the winter yet.

Stay here, keep me sane, stay stay here.

Soon the coats will go on sale at Old Navy.

Don't stop. keep me *here*, this keeps me sane.
stop. stop. keep me here.
stop. keep me here. no please. stop.
stop. keep me here with the birds.

They haven't left Pittsburgh yet. The birds!
They are waiting.

Coats will go on sale at Old Navy.

Keep me here where my feet are on the ground clearing the pebbles.

Keep me *here* with every foot fall on the path -

every foot scrape on the path is new on this Sunday morning in mid September and there are birds birds birds birds birds

This city can't stop popping from tunnels!
She thinks

    she is losing her brother

thinks of losing her lovers   and
stands on a cement block above the park.

Here, in Pittsburgh, people are left
standing.

Here below St. Paul's Cathedral, below the church
on Neville.

Arms raised, hands shaped to dive,

                                        no

 frantic hands open.

I tore the plastic package off a banana
nut muffin this morning:

> They're working on the church with the
> red doors,
> did you see it too?

> *I was wearing clothes! Stop asking.*

> I was wearing my tennis shoes which are
> gray—
> oh and my Santa Cruz sweatshirt.
> It was about 60 degrees out and
> the trees are turning. They aren't turned
> yet.

> The guys parked their trucks on the lawn
> with white paper tucked under the back
> tires and blocked my usual path.

> I ate bread on the steps of the church
> and watched two squirrels fight from
> the top of a birch all the way down to the
> bottom and all the way to the top again.
> I feel too tired to tell you more, please be
> patient.

Fall

You can turn right onto Craig street, but if the light is green go
towards Neville. Yellow light: run. Pass Mitchell's Tavern.
Cross here or in the middle later. You will not pass the Obama
poster.

Walk to the end where the church sits on the corner:

The Church of Ascension

Walk through the parking lot. A Salt Works van sits here.

Don't touch the church, not yet.

Don't touch the church, touch is too much.

Please, please, the columns are *wet paint* don't touch.
I know - I know the column - don't touch -

Left left left and there's a patch with heads
of trees above a circle of grass.

Kneel there. Wait for me.

In the fall the hills are—
two times a day I pass the apartment on Bayard
and rub my body against the Obama poster.
Obama, Biden, Bayard
Banana muffins   Pittsburgh
mornings!

Has it been more than forty days?
Do you remember your body in her hands? Her
hard hands that are dull brown calloused and
scrape your penis until

                              I can't take it no more.

You've never had hands like hers! They taste
like onions and can grip tomatoes. They peel like
onions/burnt almond body.

I am beneath you, remember? I am soft now,
watch me touch these bodies, look! I am soft now,
softest when I touch parking meters.

This morning   this morning   this
morning

I perched on a stoop at the same church

I told you about the church, don't argue.

This morning I perched on the steps of the
church,

I told you about it, didn't I?

Cross-legged and late to work

under the hardwood sky.

I stared at the growing, itty pines.
Their cylindrical bodies rose   rose
rose
They spread their arms towards my face,
so I dug my nose into the bead green pine.
I dug my face in it.

I already told you, my face was in the pine,

under the hardwood floor sky

Winter

When they put the long video
recording device into my vagina
they did not ask if it hurt or not. Is
that odd?

They flipped the switch and pushed
their hands down on my belly
and I winced so quietly,

> I winced and it was so loud
>   that they stopped,
>   but did
>   not ask anything.

There was a screen and it was green,

There was a screen and it was   It
made me wince to see my insides out
here in the open

reality tv.

*Look, you are twenty-something years
old and you have your insides
out here in the open!*

I lift my top above my tits to make the
scene complete.

Start on Bigelow Blvd and Centre Avenue.

Face
Schenley
High School.

Cross the street at the light.
Check your watch, 7:35 am.
You have plenty of time, don't worry -

I'm not.

Once you've crossed, walk down the hill.
Ice will make this difficult.

Don't worry, I'm not going to slip, ignore me.

Walk past the boy waiting at the bus stop
slick with a sweater vest and not cold, like you.

26

Today,

When I walked back from bloodborne pathogens
at Benedum Hall, I stopped the wrong stop   missed the
church, took a turn, and ran into your Wednesday afternoon thoughts.

I heard you before the snow began to fall.

I am surprised to find this crisp
memory like snow   gorgeous and

r   o   u   n   d   in my mouth.

Here's a picture of me
drawing a picture of me
drawing a picture of men

Can you pull your body from me, please? I can't do this now.

I'm very congested today.   B l o c k e d .
I haven't sat at the steps of the church,
not because I don't want to

                                                    You know I do

My nasal passages are heavy with warm, watery mucus.

Instead,

I sat beneath my window and feel it trickle   drip.

Who knows? If the Pacific sat at my feet
and you and
                              I were alone,
I might build a house of stone
for you.
For you
for you you you you.

A house of stone for you.

12.13.08 0900: Hy old mancan you give me a ride to the doctor's again? I need to get blood work done

12.13.08 1135: No prob babe, what time.

And when you found me on the bed I was sprawled.
You said my legs looked like they did when we sat at Panther
Pond and mosquitoes ate all of me.

When you found me here in my bed, you found me and felt my
forehead and here it goes again:

When they put the heavy-metal-plastic-covered vest on my
chest to take an x-ray, I thought of you.

Laughed when she said *hold still* the way I wriggle beneath
your body.

We have had a lot of good days, today might have been a good
day.

Schenley park is so far gone now. Gray gray sky gray gray low
gray sky.

They found a cyst today, I thought of you.
They found another cyst, the old ones are still—
they found a cyst today, I thought of you the way you looked—
I looked at you from a yellow cab, your cap bobbing on Baum
blvd.

They found a cyst today and it was round and bobbing on
the monitor, it leaned on my ovary like your head on my
shoulder.

I swing the creaking swing in Schenley and watch UPMC
in the foreground with a gloved hand on my belly.

Do you have family here? No.
Can someone pick you up from the hospital? I can walk.
Do you have friends? One.
Can he pick you up? Not today.

They found a cyst today and I laughed as I walked into the
Saturday morning sun in winter cold air caught in throat and I
am tickled. They found a cyst today sitting on my ovary, resting
on - drooping on.

I thought of you my my my my my Mister.
I thought of you when they found a cyst and snapped
the bracelet on my wrist

In the bedroom
the curve of your arm   to shoulder
we wait for the weather   to tender
my body dropping from the light   cover

My skin is shifting this morning - impressionable like

ice

like

sidewalks in North Oakland.

Take your hand and move it out of your world—

out of the woods more west than where we are.

Move it along my side.

Where are you?

Is your mouth F I L L E D with another's hair?

Straight, sleek.

Not overbearing.

Not coarse,

long and black.

So black it's blue.

This winter is long,   a Pittsburgh winter.
I'm waiting for the weather   to tender
waiting for a reason   to meander
                  to touch the trees,

to catch my hair in the chain swing in Schenley.

Is this on? Can you hear me? When they put
the audio recording device in   my vagina they asked me if
          it is
okay and I said NO IT IS NOT but   they needed a sound byte—
          A sound bite to
my nipples would have made the scene   complete, but they
          were gloved and masked and all
he did was brush inside/ side / side / side

You and me, Cassandra, dance [among the] dead
branches of the mid-winter frost. Where   *they*
left you, I find solace.   In your wide   mouth—
your disgusting countenance and proud   breasts.
In this city, I sit on buses   and
here you are among the black children   and
brown fingers grasping at silver handrails.
You and me are too weak to be alone.

Not yet. Do not leave, Cassandra, Let's find
him among the rest   *okay*   Rest.   No rest.
[   ]   [   ]   [Jeffers]
[
in the salt pi]es   [   ]   [   ]
in the   fleetingsalt   piles
in this   c   i   t   y

Spring

Standing on the curb denotes brink.
The church had two doors open! Two red doors!

There are men   men   men   men
at the Church of Ascension!
There are machines and
automatonic sounds blurring behind headsets!

Rusted scaffolds lean against the black church scraping
themselves clean in the wind! And the scaffolding is dotted
with   men   men   men   men

Straddle a tree
w green-centered
leaves: a maple.

Stink bugs crawl from one edge of the ceiling to the other.

It seemed like it was going to be a good day today,
not gray, not gray.

Here in Pittsburgh <twilight bounds softly>

where snow doesn't break for,

no, this ain't no James Wright poem.
no, no ma.

She can't break,
She can't break
She can't   bop into blossom.

Are you proud?

On my knees.

Looking up at your   rough chin.
                        open mouthed like

a sparrow, sparrow   s   par   ro   roud   proud of me?

Open gullet   wait

I picked up my bike from the bi   ke shop
from the bbuh ike shop.   I picked up my bike
from the shop today and rode it in the rain
in the Pittsburgh

rain. The front of my peach tank top was soaked and cinched in
my triangle crotch my cunt - tucked dress sopping wet
        I straddled the seat and remembered you when you
fixed my pipes

yellow clogged bathtub
you sat, I straddled the rim rim tub rim
tub rim of the tub.

You asked me for a paper towel, I gave you this:
you laid me down, mister
and moved your hands from my toes to my neon
clitoris.

My lips suck skin
like my blue sweater soaked
with rain water.

Get my tub again soon.

sure babe   I'm in squirrel hill, be there in fifteen

You once told me that you loved the me who writes and
       the me who's wrecked.

When my nose is at your pelvis and you dip down into my
throat. Which woman is wincing?

Which woman's dark eyes are watching your lips curl,
pushing your hand to place a tighter grip at the base of her
neck?

You— YOU
take your dirty hands and smear my brown tits

you
lick my dark nipples and my eyes watch your lips
lips
your lips lips watch two lips purse and separate.

You
take your long, smudged fingers and wipe the mess from
today on my body and my face bends
bends it bends

towards Pittsburgh looking for the city lights
in empty empty streets

Bodies with legs that meet at a point
like the
Monongahela and the Allegheny.

My mouth is   this morning this morning   I cup
my breasts and hope that you will push your way in again.

When you drive past my apartment do you see me watching the
yellow yellow buds of this Pittsburgh spring?

They pull themselves from the matrix of skin, from bulge twig,
the yellow buds break. Pop from their matrices and forget that these
breaks are hard -

so laugh.

Did you wait all day like me? You drive through the Liberty tunnels
and wait for this city to pop, you stop on the side of the
             road and think of me?

The way I looked / you looked at me from the tree beside my window.
Oh the trees!

Pittsburgh, I've missed you. Where have you been?
Tucked beneath the curtain of gray?

Oh Pittsburgh! When you jumped from out the tunnel
I forgot to watch closely. You see, I was—nothing.

I am lost. Do you forgive me, city?
You were waiting beside the tree,

waiting for me to see the city beneath the gray.
You tell me things. You held me here on my red sofa.

So farfar away. I dream of taking a bus to your house, standing
beneath your trees and shouting at the city

please please please love me.

I've faced the lilac tulips towards the french windows
and like ears   they listen. If we lay in my bed we
can see the tips sip sipping rain/sun through the dingy
screen through rectangles through smells of compost
if you lay in my bed / rest in my bed you can see the
tulips living through geometric space and dust and sun
and rest, you can see this, just face west.

what's up i miss u

been working hard girl

want me to make some dinner
i will feed you, you work too hard old man

i can't, we have plans tonight

i can feed you in other ways

i can be late

you say *you look naked* and I say
my dear say say my dear say my dear

When you stop in my apartment I
offer you food,
you say *I'm okay* I say stay stay I say
stay

When you walk up my stairs I say
*stay good man stay place your fingers
here*—
you lay in my bed and I turn around
on top of you—
my clit rubbing the soft bulge of your
tan body.

I rock myself to sleep, you turn me,
curl me in your arms
to rest my thighs and keep the pulse
of my working body from bursting.

When you curled your fingers around
the base of my neck
I push my face into your pelvis.

I don't wince—
I'm used to this.

I found Jesus Christ today when I walked past St. Paul's
Cathedral on Fifth and Craig. It was dark out, and you said
Pittsburgh's safe, but Jesus scared me half to death!

I had two toes in the church when I remembered your body
on mine   growling above me - my mom said when you
sleep with one man you get his demons.

Go ahead - g r o w l. I'll crawl into the church when my
body is ready and my soul is the color of holy water.

Today I went to sit on the steps of the church, but was
blocked.
 The cavalcade stopped at the red doors with eyes on their
            fore—

I stopped to look at all the white faces -
black crosses on their
            fore-

I stopped to look - and the silver, maple birch trees were
peeling from the long winter. Peeling their bark
tender.

I brush up against them   *and*
you?

You're home with your family.

Here I am watching the crosses bear down on the bodies of
white people in front of this church.

They have dots on their faces.
They stain the cement, but don't look down.

—heads
—heads

I wait for you   sit in the middle of the bed   touching fingers to chin
          you on my right   and him on my left *see?*

Who has made an idol of me?

You sit on my left and he sits on my right, we three huddle under the
wings of an angel and wait for the flames that lick our   faces
retreat.

Call me
faithful-
call me
faithful-

call me

Late Spring

Thank you for the bike map.
I found the map helpful -
I was lost in Liberty.

My bike is in the shop,
but the map is better than the grid
bitmap
I get from Google.

Did you crawl beneath a building
today?
Hook pipes together?
Fix water problems?

I tried to put the basket on the bike today,
Father.
I bought the basket from the men, from the
men at Iron City Bikes. This city is.
This city is. Meaty.
I rode my bike home with the basket
sticking from my pack.

I cried when I carried the heavy bike up my
spiral steps.
Can you see this city?
Little girl city?

She is breached. Her feet are coming first,
her head is lost - her head with the basket
carrying in the backpack.

You found me here, you stopped the truck   stopped
short.
You found me here, you stopped the truck.   From ocean
mouth you dragged the rocks.   A
valley,
A cypress.   I planted me.
Pittsburgh eats me.
Did you see me in this dress?
Fill your mouth.

I walked to Schenley park today   the weather was, *yes*,
okay.
One foot fall and then the next I heard your *ping*

looked down to see a text

Rough days?
—AND?

The sky beyond the conservatory
was cornflower   cornflower   cornflower
cornflower blue behind white   cornflower glass.

Like tiny pelicans the soft-edged crosses
of the conservatory roof sang —no-echo your *ping*
Your soft *ping*   soft *ping*   between cornflower *ping.*

We are a pelican song. We are a soft whistle. We are

nothing really

Dear Pittsburgh,

There are times when you look at me—I don't
see you - you see me. You come from out the
tunnel. You drive beyond the yellow church.
I sat there today   did you see me?

There are times when I think of you so far
away in a place that is   gray—
I am here   and   there you are
We've been here before:

When you come into my bed, you watch my light—you say: *you look
good naked*, I say stay.
I say my dear say say my dear say dear.
I offer you food, you say *I'm okay.*

You're tired
                    I say,

and worn
                    I say   *good*
  man stay stay I say stay
                    say stay stay good.

65

About the Poet

Rachelle Escamilla is the proud descendant of campesinos and cholos. She is the producer and host of the longest running poetry radio show in the United States, Out of Our Minds (KKUP) and the founder of the Poets & Writers Coalition at San Jose State University. From 2012-2014 Rachelle lived in China where she co-founded The Sun Yat-sen University English-language Center for Creative Writing and headed a lecture series at the American Center of the United States Consulate of Guangzhou. She is the winner of the Virginia de Arujo Academy of American Poets prize and she teaches Creative Writing and Social Action at California State University Monterey Bay. In 2018, Rachelle was a Visiting Scholar at the Library of Congress, Hispanic Division, where she conducted research around her grandfather's 1969 testimony for the fair treatment of migrant laborers in California and recorded poems for the library's archive. Rachelle was born and raised in Hollister, California and currently lives in Monterey, California.

Additional Praise for *me drawing a picture of me[n]*

In me drawing a picture of me[n], Rachelle Escamilla deftly captures the all-at-once-ness that is the basis of ecstacy in an ordinary life—when the threshold states of elation, despair and unknowing are experienced in rapid succession, alternating, blurring and at times joining together so that a person finds themself wrenched by sensations and standing outside themself, observing themself as they are touched exquisitely or ruthlessly by the people, localities and predicaments shaping their particular fate. Here it is the American city of Pittsburgh, where the foundational American problems of racial injustice, poverty, and political reckoning (or lackthereof), meet the universals of love, desire, natural beauty and religious peril in the body of the Chicana speaker, whose voice touches every register in its compelling address.

—Adam Soldofsky, Memory Foam, 2017 American Book Award Winner

In Rachelle Escamilla's remarkable second book, me drawing a picture of me[n], the personal becomes powerfully and inextricably linked to an interpersonal lyric that strikes at the roots of (economic and male) malfeasance and toxic masculinity. Staged as four seasons in the city of Pittsburgh during the momentous election year of 2008, this complex book scours the cityscape for signs of permanence—some more illusory or sophistic than others—against a backdrop of transience and shimmering hope. Escamilla writes, "Here I am searching this city for fundamentals but finding lost / words like: beauty, sublime, or lascivious innuendo." That these terms are fraught with the historical pollution of (white) male perspectives is part of Escamilla's project, as she skillfully pieces together a dense portraiture of failed encounters, broken correspondences, and emotional contusions. Escamilla reconstructs the city from inside through its exits and disappearances. Between rituals of ascension and declension, me drawing a picture of me(n) chronicles the shifting apparatus of institutionalized poverty, illness, abuse, heartbreak, and renewal from the standpoint of a lyrical vulnerability that does not speak so much as reinscribes the self.

—Jose-luis Moctezuma, Place-Discipline, 2018 Omnidawn Prize Winner

CPSIA information can be obtained
at www.ICGtesting.com
Printed in the USA
FSHW011644150319
56413FS